S0-ASN-208

God's Lite
Chicken Soup™

---

for the *Spirit*

STARBURST **PUBLISHERS**™

P.O. Box 4123, Lancaster, Pennsylvania 17604

Credits:

Cover art by David Marty Design.
Illustration by Bill Dussinger.
Scripture Quotations are from The Holy Bible:
King James Version,
New International Version, Copyright 1984 by The International Bible Society and
    published by Zondervan Bible Publishers,
New American Standard Bible, Copyright 1988 by the Lockman Foundation.

We, the Publisher and Authors, declare that to the best of our knowledge all material
(quoted or not) contained herein is accurate; and we shall not be held liable for the same.

GOD'S LITE CHICKEN SOUP FOR THE SPIRIT

First Printing, March 1996

ISBN: 0-914984-77-2
Library of Congress Catalog Number 95-71944

Printed in the United States of America

God's Lite Chicken Soup for the Spirit is a collection of inspirational Quotes and Scriptures by many of your favorite Christian speakers and writers. It will motivate your life and inspire your spirit. You will *de-lite* in the wisdom of each spoonful of ***God's Lite Chicken Soup for the Spirit.***

A heartfelt thanks to all the Starburst staff, Kathy Collard Miller and D. Larry Miller, and Pastor Steve Hammer for their efforts in compiling this keepsake.

Be sure to read ***God's Chicken Soup for the Spirit:*** *"Tug-at-the-Heart" Stories to Motivate Your Life and Inspire Your Spirit* (see next page for ordering information).

The companion book to *God's Lite Chicken Soup for the Spirit.*

God's Chicken Soup for the Spirit

Kathy Collard Miller & D. Larry Miller

Subtitled: *Tug-at-the-Heart Stories to Motivate Your Life and Inspire Your* Spirit.
Includes inspiring stories and anecdotes that emphasize Christian ideals
  and values by Barbara Johnson, Billy Graham, Nancy L. Dorner,
  Dave Dravecky, Patsy Clairmont, Charles Swindoll, H. Norman Wright,
  Adell Harvey, Max Lucado, James Dobson, Jack Hayford and many other
  well-known Christian speakers and writers.
Topics include: Love, Family Life, Faith and Trust, Prayer, Marriage,
  Relationships, Grief, Spiritual Life, Perseverance, Christian Living,
  and God's Guidance.

ISBN 0914984764 TP $12.95

God's *Lite* Chicken Soup for the Spirit

ISBN 0914984772 TP $6.95

Purchasing Information:
Books are available from your favorite Bookstore, either from current stock or special order. To assist
bookstore in locating your selection be sure to give title, author, and ISBN #. If unable to purchase
from the bookstore you may order direct from STARBURST PUBLISHERS. When ordering enclose
full payment plus $3.00 for shipping and handling ($4.00 if Canada or Overseas). Payment in US
Funds only. Please allow two to three weeks minimum (longer overseas) for delivery. Make checks
payable to and mail to STARBURST PUBLISHERS, P.O. Box 4123, LANCASTER, PA 17604. Credit
card orders may also be placed by calling 1-800-441-1456 (credit card orders only), Mon-Fri,
8 AM–5 PM Eastern Time. **Prices subject to change without notice.**   10-95

God has no problems, only plans.

–Corrie ten Boom

The LORD foils the plans of the nations; he thwarts the purposes of the peoples. But the plans of the LORD stand firm forever, the purposes of his heart through all generations.

Psalm 33:10,11 NIV

Too many people are praying for mountains of difficulty to be removed, when what they really need is courage to climb them.

But they that wait upon the LORD shall renew their strength; they shall mount up with wings as eagles; they shall run, and not be weary; and they shall walk, and not faint.

Isaiah 40:31

Experience is always the hardest teacher, because you take the test before you learn your lesson.

For a just man falleth seven times, and riseth up again . . .
Proverbs 24:16a

Any fool can count the seeds in an apple. Only God can count all the apples in one seed.

–*Robert Schuller*

Look at the birds of the air; they do not sow or reap or store away in barns, and yet your heavenly Father feeds them. Are you not much more valuable than they?

Matthew 6:26 NIV

If nothing in this world satisfies me, perhaps it is because I was made for another world.

–C. S. Lewis

But our citizenship is in heaven. And we eagerly await a Savior from there, the Lord Jesus Christ . . .

Philippians 3:20 NIV

It is practically a law of life that when one door closes on us, another opens. The trouble is that we often look with so much regret and longing upon the closed door that we do not see the one which has opened for us.

A man's steps are directed by the LORD. How then can anyone understand his own way?

Proverbs 20:24 NIV

**Worry pulls tomorrow's cloud
over today's sunshine.**

*Therefore do not worry about tomorrow, for tomorrow
will worry about itself. Each day has enough trouble of its
own.*

Matthew 6:34 NIV

The Christian life is not a 100-yard dash. It is a marathon.

–Steve Farrar

Brethren, I count not myself to have apprehended: but this one thing I do, forgetting those things which are behind, and reaching forth unto those things which are before, I press toward the mark for the prize of the high calling of God in Christ Jesus.

Philippians 3:13,14

A successful man is one who can lay a firm foundation with the bricks others have thrown at him.

–*Sherri Melsby*

In God, whose word I praise, In God I have put my trust; I shall not be afraid. What can mere man do to me?

Psalm 56:4 NASB

 **The picture of health requires a happy frame of mind.**

A merry heart doeth good like a medicine: but a broken spirit drieth the bones.

Proverbs 17:22

To bring up a child in the way he should go, travel that way yourself once in a while.

–Josh Billings

Train up a child in the way he should go: and when he is old, he will not depart from it.

Proverbs 22:6

Sometimes the Lord calms the storm, sometimes He lets the storm rage and calms His child.

Let the beloved of the LORD rest secure in him, for he shields him all day long, and the one the LORD loves rests between his shoulders.

Deuteronomy 33:12 NIV

God doesn't come when you want Him, but he's right on time.

–Tennessee Williams

Why art thou cast down, O my soul? and why art thou disquieted in me? Hope thou in God: for I shall yet praise him for the help of his countenance.

Psalm 42:5

Many pray, not to ascertain God's will, but to get His approval of their own.

When you ask, you do not receive, because you ask with wrong motives, that you may spend what you get on your pleasures.

James 4:3 NIV

The difficulties of life are intended to make us better, not bitter.

Therefore I am well content with weaknesses, with insults, with distresses, with persecutions, with difficulties, for Christ's sake; for when I am weak, then I am strong.

2 Corinthians 12:10 NASB

If you own something you cannot give away, then you don't own it, it owns you.

–Albert Schweitzer

Not that I speak in respect of want: for I have learned, in whatsoever state I am, therewith to be content.

Philippians 4:11

It is wonderful what God can do with the broken heart, if He gets all the pieces.

The crucible for silver and the furnace for gold, but the LORD tests the heart.

Proverbs 17:3 NIV

Those who travel the high road of humility are not troubled by heavy traffic.

–Alan K. Simpson

Humble yourselves in the sight of the Lord, and he shall lift you up.

James 4:10

There is a world of difference between knowing the Word of God and knowing the God of the Word.

–Leonard Ravenhill

That I may know him, and the power of his resurrection, and the fellowship of his sufferings, being made conformable unto his death . . .

Philippians 3:10

God is more interested in making us what we ought to be than in giving us what we think we ought to have.

So we fix our eyes not on what is seen, but on what is unseen. For what is seen is temporary, but what is unseen is eternal.

2 Corinthians 4:18 NIV

Everything depends on our being right in Christ. If I want good apples, I must have a good apple tree.

–Andrew Murray

A good man out of the good treasure of the heart bringeth forth good things: and an evil man out of the evil treasure bringeth forth evil things.

Matthew 12:35

God never alters the robe of righteousness to fit the man; He changes the man to fit the robe.

He will keep you strong to the end, so that you will be blameless on the day of our Lord Jesus Christ.

1 Corinthians 1:8 NIV

If you don't have enough time for your family, you can be 100% certain you are not following God's will for your life.

–Patrick M. Morley

But if any provide not for his own, and specially for those of his own house, he hath denied the faith, and is worse than an infidel.

1 Timothy 5:8

When you pray for God's guidance, do not complain if it is different from your preference.

This is the confidence we have in approaching God: that if we ask anything according to his will, he hears us.

1 John 5:14 NIV

Live as though Christ died yesterday, rose from the grave today, and is coming back tomorrow.

–Theodore Epp

Therefore keep watch, because you do not know on what day your Lord will come.

Matthew 24:42 NIV

God doesn't want you busy about everything, but He does want you busy about something. He even knows what it is.

–Patricia Sprinkle

For we are his workmanship, created in Christ Jesus unto good works, which God hath before ordained that we should walk in them.

Ephesians 2:10

A gossiper is like an old shoe . . . its tongue never stays in place.

Whoso keepeth his mouth and his tongue keepeth his soul from troubles.

Proverbs 21:23

Patience is the ability to count down before blasting off!

A soft answer turneth away wrath: but grievous words stir up anger.

Proverbs 15:1

Prayer does more than help us get what we want, it helps us become what God wants.

And we, who with unveiled faces all reflect the Lord's glory, are being transformed into his likeness with ever-increasing glory, which comes from the Lord, who is the Spirit.

2 Corinthians 3:18 NIV

Kindness is Christianity with its working clothes on.

What is desirable in a man is his kindness . . .

Proverbs 19:22a NASB

Living from hand to mouth is not so bad when it's God's hand.

For with God nothing shall be impossible.

Luke 1:37

A candle loses nothing of its light by lighting another candle.

And if you give yourself to the hungry, And satisfy the desire of the afflicted, Then your light will rise in darkness, And your gloom will become like midday.

Isaiah 58:10 NASB

**If you're going to step on toes,
wear bedroom slippers.**

–Liz Curtis Higgs

. . . speaking the truth in love. . .

Ephesians 4:15

I do not like crises, but I do like the opportunities they supply.

—William Barclay

Behold, I will do a new thing; now it shall spring forth; shall ye not know it? I will even make a way in the wilderness, and rivers in the desert.

Isaiah 43:19

God mightily uses Christians who stay cool in a hot place, sweet in a sour place, and little in a big place.

A man's discretion makes him slow to anger, And it is his glory to overlook a transgression.

Proverbs 19:11 NASB

Real charity doesn't care if it's tax-deductible or not.

–Dan Bennett

Religion that God our Father accepts as pure and faultless is this: to look after orphans and widows in their distress and to keep oneself from being polluted by the world.

James 1:27 NIV

Other people don't create your spirit; they only reveal it.

–Henry Brandt

Wherefore let him that thinketh he standeth take heed lest he fall.

1 Corinthians 10:12

Experience is what you get when you don't get what you want.

–*Dan Stanford*

. . . so that you may walk in a manner worthy of the Lord, to please Him in all respects, bearing fruit in every good work and increasing in the knowledge of God . . .

Colossians 1:10 NASB

There is only one thing for a man to do who is married to a woman who enjoys spending money, and that is to enjoy earning it.

–*E. W. Howe*

As goods increase, so do those who consume them. And what benefit are they to the owner except to feast his eyes on them?

Ecclesiastes 5:11 NIV

With God, even when nothing is happening—something is happening.

–Reubin Welch

Now unto him that is able to do exceeding abundantly above all that we ask or think, according to the power that worketh in us . . .

Ephesians 3:20

A glimpse is not a vision. But to a man on a mountain road by night, a glimpse of the next three feet of road may matter more than a vision of the horizon.

–C. S. Lewis

Make level paths for your feet and take only ways that are firm.

Proverbs 4:26 NIV

Those who walk with God always get to their destination.

The LORD will watch over your coming and going both now and forevermore.

Psalm 121:8 NIV

Our weakness becomes strength when we depend upon God to carry the heavy end.

–Joe R. Barnett

And he said unto me, My grace is sufficient for thee: for my strength is made perfect in weakness.

2 Corinthians 12:9a

The Lord can handle our anger. I'm sure He prefers to bear it rather than have us dump it on someone else or turn it in upon ourselves and be depressed.

–Tony Campolo

Cast all your anxiety on him because he cares for you.
1 Peter 5:7 NIV

It is far better to forgive and forget than to resent and remember.

And forgive us our debts, as we forgive our debtors.

Matthew 6:12

Worry does not empty tomorrow of its sorrow; it empties today of its strength.

–Corrie ten Boom

The one who received the seed that fell among the thorns is the man who hears the word, but the worries of this life and the deceitfulness of wealth choke it, making it unfruitful.

Matthew 13:22 NIV

**God wants men great enough
to be small enough to be used.**

*Therefore in Christ Jesus I have found reason for boasting
in things pertaining to God. For I will not presume to
speak of anything except what Christ has accomplished
through me. . .*

Romans 15:17,18 NASB

Try praising your wife, even if it frightens her at first.

–Billy Sunday

Her children arise up, and call her blessed; her husband also, and he praiseth her.

Proverbs 31:28

The next time you are called to suffer, pay attention. It may be the closest you'll ever get to God.

–*Max Lucado*

For this reason I also suffer these things, but I am not ashamed; for I know whom I have believed and I am convinced that He is able to guard what I have entrusted to Him until that day.

2 Timothy 1:12 NASB

To reach the port of heaven, we must sail, sometimes with the wind, sometimes against it, but we must sail, not drift or lie at anchor.

–Oliver Wendall Holmes

Holding faith, and a good conscience; which some having put away concerning faith have made shipwreck . . .

1 Timothy 1:19

Our children are the only earthly possessions we can take with us to glory.

Even so it is not the will of your Father which is in heaven, that one of these little ones should perish.

Matthew 18:14

**Forgiveness is no longer allowing
what has happened to poison you.**

–H. Norman Wright

*Bear with each other and forgive whatever grievances
you may have against one another. Forgive as the Lord
forgave you.*

Colossians 3:13 NIV

The secret to happiness is not in getting more but in wanting less.

–Elaine St. James

But if we have food and clothing, we will be content with that.

1 Timothy 6:8 NIV

Be assured that if God waits longer than you wish, it is only to make the blessing all the more precious.

–Andrew Murray

O LORD, thou art my God; I will exalt thee, I will praise thy name; for thou hast done wonderful things; thy counsels of old are faithfulness and truth.

Isaiah 25:1

To realize the worth of the anchor, we need to feel the storm.

When I am afraid, I will trust in you.

Psalm 56:3 NIV

Acquiring the Lord's attitude requires listening to His inner voice.

–Lloyd John Ogilvie

Be still, and know that I am God . . .

Psalm 46:10

Tears begin your healing process, and laughter propels it along.

–Barbara Johnson

Then was our mouth filled with laughter, and our tongue with singing . . .

Psalm 125:2

The secret of patience, is to do something else in the meantime.

You too, be patient and stand firm, because the Lord's coming is near.

James 5:8 NIV

Remember that the faith that moves mountains always carries a pick.

Even so faith, if it hath not works, is dead, being alone.

James 2:17

Experience enables you to recognize a mistake every time you repeat it.

But examine everything carefully; hold fast to that which is good . . .

1 Thessalonians 5:21 NASB

The kind of successor I may get may depend a great deal on the kind of predecessor I've been.

Study to show thyself approved unto God, a workman that needeth not to be ashamed, rightly dividing the word of truth.

2 Timothy 2:15

Burn on, instead of burning out.

–*Jill Briscoe*

Neither do men light a candle, and put it under a bushel,
but on a candlestick; and it giveth light unto all that are in
the house.

Matthew 5:15

No cloud comes into your life but that God has put a rainbow in it.

I have set my rainbow in the clouds, and it will be the sign of the covenant between me and the earth.

Genesis 9:13 NIV

One of the loveliest uses for imagination is to put ourselves in the place of other people, thereby being better able to see how to help them.

–Hannah Hurnard

Carry each other's burdens, and in this way you will fulfill the law of Christ.

Galatians 6:2 NIV

Where God's finger points, there God's hand will make the way.

I will instruct thee and teach thee in the way which thou shalt go: I will guide thee with mine eye.

Psalm 32:8

**God always provides enough
time to accomplish God's plans.**

–Patrick M. Morley

*To every thing there is a season, and a time to every
purpose under the heaven . . .*

Ecclesiastes 3:1

Obstacles are what you see when you take your eyes off the goal.

Perseverance must finish its work so that you may be mature and complete, not lacking anything.

James 1:4 NIV

Although God demands a whole heart, He will accept a broken one if He gets all the pieces.

Trust in him at all times; ye people, pour out your heart before him: God is a refuge for us.

Psalm 62:8

God speaks to those who take time to listen.

I waited patiently for the LORD; and he inclined unto me, and heard my cry.

Psalm 40:1

**You never get a busy signal
when you want to talk to God.**

*And call upon Me in the day of trouble; I shall rescue you,
and you will honor Me.*

Psalm 50:15 NASB

God's grace keeps pace with whatever we face.

And God is able to make all grace abound toward you; that ye, always having all sufficiency in all things, may abound to every good work . . .

2 Corinthians 9:8

Get untracked, and ontrack for God.

–Jeff Brawner

He who trusts in his own heart is a fool, But he who walks wisely will be delivered.

Proverbs 28:26 NASB

**If I do not stand for something,
I will fall for anything.**

But let him ask in faith, nothing wavering. For he that wavereth is like a wave of the sea driven with the wind and tossed.

James 1:6

A fugitive is one who is running from home. A vagabond is one who has no home. A stranger is one away from home. And a PILGRIM is on his way home.

And if I go and prepare a place for you, I will come again, and receive you unto myself; that where I am, there ye may be also.

John 14:3

The next time the devil reminds you of your past—remind him of his future.

And the devil that deceived them was cast into the lake of fire and brimstone, where the beast and the false prophet are, and shall be tormented day and night for ever and ever.

Revelation 20:10

Human beings, like chickens, thrive best when they have to scratch for what they get.

He who gathers crops in summer is a wise son, but he who sleeps during harvest is a disgraceful son.

Proverbs 10:5 NIV

**The only purposes that will
survive are the ones linked
to God.**

–Patrick M. Morley

*There are many devices in a man's heart; nevertheless the
counsel of the LORD, that shall stand.*

Proverbs 19:21

I've discovered that good evangelism does not require great theological knowledge. But evangelism definitely does require prayer.

–Becky Tirabassi

And pray for us, too, that God may open a door for our message, so that we may proclaim the mystery of Christ . . .

Colossians 4:3 NIV

There is no pit so deep that He is not deeper still.

—*Corrie ten Boom*

He brought me up also out of an horrible pit, out of the miry clay, and set my feet upon a rock, and established my goings.

Psalm 40:2,3

**The will of God will never lead
you where the grace of God cannot
keep you.**

*Behold, the eye of the LORD is upon them that fear him,
upon them that hope in his mercy . . .*

Psalm 33:18

The true function of a preacher is to disturb the comfortable and to comfort the disturbed.

As ye know how we exhorted and comforted and charged every one of you, as a father doth his children . . .

1 Thessalonians 2:11

A lot of kneeling will keep you in good standing with God.

Let us then approach the throne of grace with confidence, so that we may receive mercy and find grace to help us in our time of need.

Hebrews 4:16 NIV

Listening is at least a third of the communication process, the other thirds being the sharing of self and the understanding that follows the listening.

–Dr. Kevin Leman

For we all stumble in many ways. If anyone does not stumble in what he says, he is a perfect man, able to bridle the whole body as well.

James 3:2 NASB

God made you as you are, in order to use you as He planned.

Now then we are ambassadors for Christ, as though God did beseech you by us: we pray you in Christ's stead, be ye reconciled to God.

2 Corinthians 5:20

People who sing their own praises, do it without accompaniment.

Let another praise you, and not your own mouth;
someone else, and not your own lips.

Proverbs 27:2 NIV

When you meet the devil, you know you are not going his way. If you never meet him, you must be going in the same direction.

He was a murderer from the beginning, not holding to the truth, for there is no truth in him. When he lies, he speaks his native language, for he is a liar and the father of lies.

John 8:44 NIV

To get nowhere, follow the crowd.

As you have therefore received Christ Jesus the Lord,
so walk ye in him . . .

Colossians 2:6

In order to learn from others, we must listen and sometimes say, "I don't know."

–Florence Littauer

He who gives an answer before he hears, It is folly and shame to him.

Proverbs 18:13 NASB

Listening is an active labor, a learned skill. False listening is waiting for the other to finish; good listening is waiting on the other while he or she speaks.

–*Walter Wangarin*

But let everyone be quick to hear; slow to speak and slow to anger . . .

James 1:19 NASB

Peace can be experienced only when we have received divine pardon—when we have been reconciled to God and when we have harmony within, with our fellow man and especially with God.

–Billy Graham

Therefore being justified by faith, we have peace with God through our Lord Jesus Christ.

Romans 5:1

Feet accustomed to the road to God can find it in the dark.

–Amy Carmichael

The steps of a good man are ordered by the LORD: and he delighteth in his way.

Psalm 37:23

God's Word is a mirror that shows our true condition.

–Lew Button

For the word of God is quick, and powerful, and sharper than any two-edged sword, piercing even to the dividing asunder of soul and spirit, and of the joints and marrow, and is a discerner of the thoughts and intents of the heart.

Hebrews 4:12

**When God permits His children
to go through the furnace,
He keeps His eye on the clock
and His hand on the thermostat.
His loving heart knows how
much and how long.**

–Warren Wiersbe

*Behold, I have refined you, but not as silver; I have tested
you in the furnace of affliction.*

Isaiah 48:10 NASB

God slowly yields the good things of the kingdom and the world to those who struggle.

–Pat Robertson

Have not I commanded thee? Be strong and of a good courage; be not afraid, neither be thou dismayed: for the Lord thy God is with thee whithersoever thou goest.

Joshua 1:9

When we understand that He is Lord of our time, we realize that interruptions are of His planning. They become opportunities to serve rather than plagues to keep us from functioning.

–Karen Burton Mains

. . . and having done all, to stand. Stand therefore . . .
Ephesians 6: 13,14

Prayer is the key of the morning and the bolt on the door at night.

Again, I tell you that if two of you on earth agree about anything you ask for, it will be done for you by my Father in heaven.

Matthew 18:19 NIV

Praise is faith expressing itself.

–Adrian Rogers

By him therefore let us offer the sacrifice of praise to God continually, that is, the fruit of our lips giving thanks to his name.

Hebrews 13:15

God writes with a pen that never blots, speaks with a tongue that never slips, and acts with a hand that never fails.

God is faithful, by whom ye were called unto the fellowship of his Son Jesus Christ our Lord.

1 Corinthians 1:9

Everything is under our power of choice, but once the choice is made, we become the servant of the choice.

–*Edwin Louis Cole*

Put to death, therefore, whatever belongs to your earthly nature: sexual immorality, impurity, lust, evil desires and greed, which is idolatry.

Colossians 3:5 NIV

God without man is still God.
Man without God is nothing.

The fool hath said in his heart, There is no God. They are corrupt, they have done abominable works, there is none that doeth good.

Psalm 14:1

Some of life's biggest disappointments come from getting what we insisted on having.

For the pagans run after all these things, and your heavenly Father knows that you need them.

Matthew 6:32 NIV

I have tried to keep things in my hands and lost them all, but what I have given into God's hands I still possess.

–Martin Luther

As sorrowful, yet alway rejoicing; as poor, yet making many rich; as having nothing, and yet possessing all things.

2 Corinthians 6:10

Somebody figured out that we have 35 million laws trying to enforce the Ten Commandments.

For this is the love of God, that we keep His commandments; and His commandments are not burdensome.

1 John 5:3 NASB

If you have not quiet in your mind, outward comfort will do no more for you than a golden slipper on a gouty foot.

Thou wilt keep him in perfect peace, whose mind is stayed on thee: because he trusteth in thee.

Isaiah 26:3

One with God is a majority.

Ye are of God, little children, and have overcome them: because greater is he that is in you, than he that is in the world.

1 John 4:4

God will forgive those who start late in life to serve Him, but He will not forgive those who quit early.

Blessed is the man that endureth temptation: for when he is tried, he shall receive the crown of life, which the Lord hath promised to them that love him.

James 1:12

Laughing at ourselves is possible when we are able to see humanity as it is—a little lower than the angels and at times only slightly higher than the apes.

–Tom Mullen

What is man, that thou art mindful of him? and the son of man, that thou visitest him? For thou hast made him a little lower than the angels, and hast crowned him with glory and honour.

Psalm 8:4,5

God does not always pay at the end of each day, but God always pays in the end.

The Rock! His work is perfect, For all His ways are just; A God of faithfulness and without injustice, Righteous and upright is He.

Deuteronomy 32:4 NASB

An opportunity is not necessarily God's open door.

–Kathy Collard Miller

Unless the LORD builds the house, its builders labor in vain. Unless the LORD watches over the city, the watchmen stand guard in vain.

Psalm 127:1 NIV

Christians, like pianos, need frequent tuning.

Being confident of this very thing, that he which hath begun a good work in you will perform it until the day of Jesus Christ . . .

Philippians 1:6

The best way to be perceived as having character is to actually possess it.

–J. W. Reed

Since we have these promises, dear friends, let us purify ourselves from everything that contaminates body and spirit, perfecting holiness out of reverence for God.

2 Corinthians 7:1 NIV

**God helps those who help others
rather than themselves.**

*All the believers were one in heart and mind. No one
claimed that any of his possessions was his own, but they
shared everything they had.*

Acts 4:32 NIV

When Helen Keller was asked if there was anything worse than being blind, she answered, "Yes! Being able to see and having no vision."

–*Tony Campolo*

Where there is no revelation, the people cast off restraint; but blessed is he who keeps the law.

Proverbs 29:18 NIV

**The brook would lose its song
if the rocks were removed.**

*The words of a man's mouth are deep waters, but the
fountain of wisdom is a bubbling brook.*

Proverbs 18:1

The Lord can be trusted—even when He can't be tracked.

–James Dobson

For my thoughts are not your thoughts, neither are your ways my ways, saith the LORD.

Isaiah 55:8

God brings men into deep waters, not to drown them, but to cleanse them.

–Abraham Lincoln

These things I have spoken unto you, that in me ye might have peace. In the world ye shall have tribulation: but be of good cheer; I have overcome the world.

John 16:33

Little things affect little minds.

As a result, we are no longer to be children, tossed here and there by waves, and carried about by every wind of doctrine, by the trickery of men, by craftiness in deceitful scheming . . .

Ephesians 4:14

If I take care of my character, my reputation will take care of itself.

–D. L. Moody

Receive us; we have wronged no man, we have corrupted no man, we have defrauded no man.

2 Corinthians 7:2

If you cannot find God, guess who's lost.

God did this so that men would seek him and perhaps reach out for him and find him, though he is not far from each one of us.

Acts 17:27 NIV

When God gives you a vision and darkness follows, wait. God will make you in accordance with the vision He has given if you will wait His time. Never try and help God fulfill His word.

–Oswald Chambers

The LORD is good unto them that wait for him, to the soul that seeketh him.

Lamentations 3:25

In times of sadness and loss, ultimately we must understand God is in control.

–Annie Chapman

Let not your heart be troubled: ye believe in God, believe also in me.

John 14:1

To focus our life in Christ, we must allow Him to become Director and Audience. The movements of our life must be choreographed by Him, performed for Him.

–Jean Fleming

Thy word is a lamp unto my feet, and a light unto my path.
Psalm 119:105

Conscience: that small part of you that feels awful while the rest of you feels great.

All of us who are mature should take such a view of things. And if on some point you think differently, that too God will make clear to you.

Philippians 3:15 NIV

God didn't intend any of us to be damaged by life's rocky hard things. But it is God's intent to convert life's tough things to blessings.

–Jack Hayford

Humble yourselves therefore under the mighty hand of God, that he may exalt you in due time . . .

1 Peter 5:6

Live so that when you tell someone you are a Christian, it confirms their suspicions instead of surprises them.

Let your light so shine before men, that they may see your good works, and glorify your Father which is in heaven.

Matthew 5:16

**Swallow your pride occasionally.
It is non-fattening.**

*A man's pride shall bring him low: but honour shall
uphold the humble in spirit.*

Proverbs 29:23

Keep on asking, He said. Keep on seeking, and keep on knocking. Don't be afraid even to make a ruckus.

–Pat Robertson

I tell you, even though he will not get up and give him anything because he is his friend, yet because of his persistence he will get up and give him as much as he needs.

Luke 11:8 NASB

If we seek God's will, and we're confident that we're acting according to His will, it's much easier to let go of worry and trust He will keep His promises.

–Annie Chapman

It is vain for you to rise up early, To retire late, To eat the bread of painful labors; For He gives to His beloved even in his sleep.

Psalm 127:2 NASB

He who serves God for money might be tempted to serve the Devil for better wages.

No one can serve two masters. Either he will hate the one and love the other, or he will be devoted to the one and despise the other. You cannot serve both God and money.

Matthew 6:24 NIV

Disappointment often focuses on the failure of our own agenda rather than on God's long-term purposes for us, which may use stress and struggle as tools for strengthening our spiritual muscles.

–*Luci Shaw*

It was good for me to be afflicted so that I might learn your decrees.

Psalm 119:71 NIV

The people in your life are like the pillars on your porch. Sometimes they hold you up, and sometimes they lean on you. Sometimes it is enough to know they're standing by.

–*Merle Shain*

. . . from whom the whole body, being fitted and held together by that which every joint supplies, according to the proper working of each individual part, causes the growth of the body for the building up of itself in love.

Ephesians 4:16 NASB

For the Christian, there's absolutely nothing morbid about the thought of death. On the contrary, it's getting ready to go visit your very best friend.

–*Ray Ortlund*

And now, little children, abide in him; that, when he shall appear, we may have confidence, and not be ashamed before him at his coming.

1 John 2:28

To keep a lamp burning we have to keep putting oil in it.

–Mother Teresa

And be renewed in the spirit of your mind; And that ye put on the new man, which after God is created in righteousness and true holiness.

Ephesians 4:23,24

To be used of God is victory, to be used of man is victimization.

–Patsy Clairmont

But thanks be to God, which giveth us the victory through our Lord Jesus Christ.

1 Corinthians 15:57 NIV

We belong to an orchestra, and we make harmony by playing our particular part of the score on the instrument given to us.

–Elizabeth Elliot

But now hath God set the members every one of them in the body, as it hath pleased him. And if they were all one member, where were the body? But now are they many members, yet but one body.

1 Corinthians 12:18–20

Don't pray about anything you wouldn't want God to do through you.

–Charles Stanley

Devote yourselves to prayer, being watchful and thankful.
Colossians 4:2 NIV

God never sends a burden to weigh us down without offering His arm to lift us up.

Come unto me, all ye that labour and are heavy laden, and I will give you rest.

Matthew 11:28

Remember, don't lose your temper, some poor soul might find it.

Starting a quarrel is like breaching a dam; so drop the matter before a dispute breaks out.

Proverbs 17:14 NIV

Moral failure is rarely the result of a blowout; almost always, it's the result of a slow leak.

–*Gary J. Oliver*

Like a bird that strays from its nest is a man who strays from his home.

Proverbs 27:8 NIV

The church is full of willing people: Some are willing to work, others are willing to let them.

Therefore, my beloved brethren, be ye steadfast, unmoveable, always abounding in the work of the Lord, forasmuch as ye know that your labour is not in vain in the Lord.

1 Corinthians 15:58

When God bolts a door, don't try to go through a window.

A man's heart deviseth his way: but the LORD directeth his steps.

Proverbs 16:9

When wealth is lost, nothing is lost; when health is lost, something is lost; but when character is lost, all is lost.

–John R. Strubhar

A good name is rather to be chosen than great riches, and loving favour rather than silver and gold.

Proverbs 22:1

Patience is never acquired from reading it in a book or observing it in the lives of others. It is the fruit of difficulty and the by-product of learning how to wait.

–*Luci Swindoll*

Wait on the LORD: be of good courage, and he shall strengthen thine heart: wait, I say, on the LORD.

Psalm 27:14

**We cannot avoid growing old,
but we can avoid growing cold.**

*And even when I am old and gray, O God, do not
forsake me, Until I declare Thy strength to this generation,
Thy power to all who are to come.*

Psalm 71:18 NASB

Too many people have a strong *will* and a weak *will not*.

But every man is tempted, when he is drawn away of his own lust, and enticed.

James 1:14

We know that a fool and his money are soon parted, but how did they ever get together in the first place?

–E. C. McKenzie

For the love of money is the root of all evil: which while some coveted after, they have erred from the faith, and pierced themselves through with many sorrows.

1 Timothy 6:10

Blessed is he who has nothing to say!

When words are many, sin is not absent, but he who holds his tongue is wise.

Proverbs 10:19 NIV

Be careful of your thoughts; they may become words at any moment.

Casting down imaginations, and every high thing that exalteth itself against the knowledge of God, and bringing into captivity every thought to the obedience of Christ . . .
2 Corinthians 10:5

Holy is the way God is. To be holy He does not conform to a standard. He is that standard.

–A. W. Tozer

For thus says the high and exalted One Who lives forever, whose name is Holy, "I dwell on a high and holy place . . ."

Isaiah 57:15 NASB

God's sovereignty is our all-wise, all-knowing God reigning in realms beyond our comprehension to bring about a plan beyond our ability to alter, hinder, or stop.

–Charles Swindoll

The LORD of hosts has sworn saying, "Surely, just as I have intended so it has happened, and just as I have planned so it will stand . . ."

Isaiah 14:24

It is never too early to begin blessing someone—even a difficult person—but we never know when it is too late.

–John Trent

Bless them which persecute you: bless, and curse not.
Romans 12:14

Sorrow looks back, worry looks around, but faith looks up.

–Charles G. Finney

Therefore we do not lose heart, but though our outer man is decaying, yet our inner man is being renewed day by day.

2 Corinthians 4:16 NASB

We are each of us angels with only one wing, and we can only fly by embracing each other.

–Luciano de Crescenzo

Greater love hath no man than this, that a man lay down his life for his friends.

John 15:13

Being on the tightrope is living; everything else is waiting.

–Karl Wallenda

I can do everything through him who gives me strength.

Philippians 4:13 NIV

To be trusted is a greater compliment than to be loved.

–George MacDonald

Trust in the LORD with all thine heart; and lean not unto thine own understanding. In all thy ways acknowledge him, and he shall direct thy paths.

Proverbs 3:5,6

I have been driven many times to my knees by the overwhelming conviction that I had nowhere else to go.

–Abraham Lincoln

. . . choose you this day whom ye will serve . . . but as for me and my house, we will serve the LORD.

Joshua 24:15